D0238200

The Story of
Trains

Jane Bingham

Illustrated by
Colin King

Reading Consultant: Alison Kelly
University of Surrey Roehampton

Contents

Chapter 1

Early engines

Hundreds of years ago, it was hard to travel from place to place. Most people walked or rode on horses. If they needed to go a long way – as far as the next town or beyond – they took a carriage.

Hop in.

But taking a carriage was dangerous. The roads were full of highwaymen, lying in wait to attack. Every passenger rode in fear of the dreaded words, "Your money or your life!"

Merchants didn't risk carriages. They used barges and sent their goods by canals. The problem with barges was their speed. It was s...l...o...w... Some took weeks to travel from one city to the next.

"We need a fast, cheap and safe way to travel!" people cried.

And then they thought, "Tracks!"
Since Roman times, every cart
driver knew his cart ran more
smoothly if it followed the tracks
made by other carts.

Keep in
the groove,
Brutus.

But horses were pulling very
heavy loads. Even using the tracks,
it was hard to pull a wagon full of
coal or iron.

Then, one day, a group of coal miners had a great idea.

"What about building iron rails for our wagons to run on?"

The rails were a huge success. But now the horses had to walk on rails and that was tricky. What was needed was an engine...

In 1712, an English blacksmith invented one. It worked using steam, only it couldn't pull a wagon so it didn't help much.

Almost a hundred years later, Richard Trevithick had the answer. Excitedly, he attached his engine to five wagons full of people.

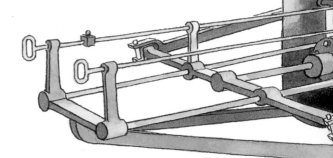

Everyone waited to see what would happen.

Slowly but surely, the engine pulled the wagons along the rails. Richard Trevithick had invented the train!

In 1808, Trevithick built a round track in London. People paid to ride in a coach pulled by his engine. It was the very first train for paying passengers.

By the 1820s,
engineers all
over Europe were
building moving
steam engines.

This beats horse power!

Some had metal teeth on their
wheels, which fitted into grooves
in the track.

Others had large wheels, which
were connected by metal rods. But
none of them ran especially well.

So, a competition was held to test different engines. Vast crowds cheered the entrants but only three reached the final.

There was the *Novelty*, which kept breaking down...

the *Sans Pareil*, which broke down after eight trips...

...and the *Rocket*, which won.

13

George Stephenson and his son
Robert, builders of the *Rocket*, were
thrilled. George had already set up
the first public rail service. It took
passengers between Stockton and
Darlington in northern England.

Soon, the Stephensons had a
factory building more engines just
like the prize-winning *Rocket*. They
became very successful, sending
their engines all over the world.

The rail companies made most
money from carrying goods, so
engineers put on their thinking
caps and designed
wagons to
carry hay...

horses...

...and
heavy
barrels.

They designed different carriages for people too.

The rich went first class, in a splendid carriage with windows and deep, soft seats.

In second class, passengers only had a hard wooden seat – but at least they had a roof over their heads.

The poorest passengers went third class. They had no roof – and often no seats – but it was quicker than walking.

Hey! My hat...

Chapter 2

Making tracks

In no time at all, people were going railway-crazy, laying rails all over Europe and North America. Rich men got together, raising money to build tracks.

Engineers planned the best routes and the builders set to work.

They spread
stones on
the ground...

laid wooden
sleepers over
the stones...

...and fitted
the rails
in place.

When the track was finished,
the rail company threw a party
for everyone who had helped.

In America, people called the new tracks "railroads". Their dream was for a railroad to cross the entire country.

In 1862, two teams of builders began work, one in the east and one in the west. For seven years, they laid rail after rail, until they finally met in Utah.

Nice to meet you at last!

Once the railroad was finished,

thousands of people went west to build farms on the open plains.

As they moved, they drove Native Americans from their

hunting grounds. The American West would never be the same.

But the rail companies had other things on their minds.

Every time a train met a hill or curve, it came off the track.

"This is hopeless!" cried the rail bosses to the engineers. "Sort it!" So they did – by inventing the bogie.

Fixed under a train's engine, the bogie could swivel from side to side, gently leading the train around curves in the track.

Then came a bigger worry. American engines burned wood, and sparks flew from their chimneys, setting passengers on fire. Engineers had to build giant chimneys to catch the sparks.

They also fixed cowcatchers to the front of trains, to push stray animals out of the way.

Back in Britain, rail companies
faced a different problem. Engineers
were using two kinds of track. Most
had the rails fairly close together,
but some tracks were wider apart.
Each track needed a different train.

All change!

When the two tracks met,
passengers had no choice. They
had to get out and change trains.
Engineers argued for fifty years
before they finally agreed to use
the narrower tracks.

Then came the biggest problem of all. So many trains were running at once that they started to crash. Signalmen had to hold up flags to warn drivers if the track was busy.

 Wooden signals soon replaced the flags and, by 1850, all the signals were worked from signal boxes.

Ten years later, signalmen used electric telegraph machines to tell each other if a train was coming.

Signalmen could also move
sections of rail at certain points,
to let trains move from one track
to another.

Neat
change!

The signalman pulled a lever
in his signal box, the track shifted
and the train puffed off in a
new direction.

Chapter 3

New challenges

More difficulties were around the corner – and some were as big as mountains. A mountain range called the Alps blocked the path of any trains trying to cross Europe. Starting on either side, teams of workmen began to dig...

They used picks, dynamite and powerful drills to blast through the rock. For fourteen years, the workmen dug and bored and blasted and dug until...

...the two sides of the tunnel joined. Between 1857 and 1922, five tunnels were built under the Alps.

Engineers were even trying to build tunnels under rivers. The tunnel under the River Severn, joining England and Wales, took over ten years to build and flooded five times before it was finished.

In some places, engineers decided to build bridges instead. If there was plenty of wood around, they built wooden bridges.

The only trouble was, wood could rot and crumble. For some creatures, it was also a tasty snack. In India, several bridges collapsed when ants ate through the wood.

The strongest bridges were made from steel. The Forth Bridge in Scotland, which is over a mile wide, was made from steel tubes.

First, workmen built three huge piers in the river. Then they joined the piers together. The first train ran across the bridge in 1890.

At last, the railways in Europe and North America were running smoothly – and other countries noticed.

"I want a railway to link the cities of Moscow and Vladivostok," declared the ruler of Russia in 1891.

The track would have to stretch for six thousand miles across icy plains and mountains, deep lakes, rivers and bogs. It was another ten years before the first train could begin the long journey.

On the way, the train met a large lake. As the lake was too wide for a bridge, a ferry carried the train to the other side.

This plan worked well until winter, when the lake froze solid.

"Aha!" cried the engineers and quickly laid rails over the ice. But before the first train was even halfway across...

...the ice cracked and the train plunged into freezing water.

Engineers had to build tracks around the lake instead. It took another three years before trains could cross Russia safely – and only the most powerful could make the long, bitterly cold journey.

Trains weren't only going over lakes and under rivers. In London, where the streets were clogged with people and traffic, they were going underground.

First, builders dug a vast hole in the street and put a roof over the top. They covered the roof with the earth they had just dug up, and then rebuilt the street on top.

Of course, while they dug, the streets couldn't be used... until Henry Greathead, an engineer, came up with the answer.

He invented a metal tube that let the builders work underground.

The first section of underground anywhere in the world opened in London in 1863.

With trains running everywhere,
architects designed
amazing stations
for them. Some
could have been
mistaken for
cathedrals
or palaces.

Many had
huge, arching
roofs of glass
and metal...

...and underground
stations in Moscow
were so grand,
they looked
like ballrooms.

Chapter 4

Riding in style

By 1850, thousands of people were using trains. This gave an American furniture maker, George Pullman, a great idea.

Why not make a train more like a home?

Before long, Pullman carriages were everywhere. During the day, the carriages had soft seats and wide corridors so the passengers could walk around.

At night, bunk beds folded down from above the seats. Even the seats themselves could be turned into beds. Thick curtains kept the beds private.

Now that carriages were so comfortable, it became very fashionable to travel by rail.

Kings, queens and presidents all rode in trains and, in 1869, a royal train was built for the British queen, Victoria. Unlike earlier trains, Queen Victoria's even had a toilet on board.

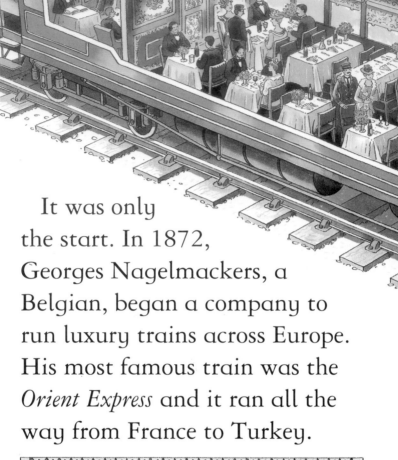

It was only
the start. In 1872,
Georges Nagelmackers, a
Belgian, began a company to
run luxury trains across Europe.
His most famous train was the
Orient Express and it ran all the
way from France to Turkey.

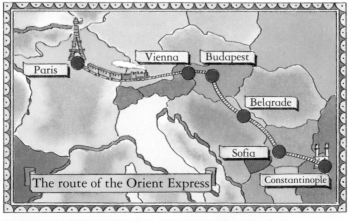

Paris
Vienna
Budapest
Belgrade
Sofia
Constantinople

The route of the Orient Express

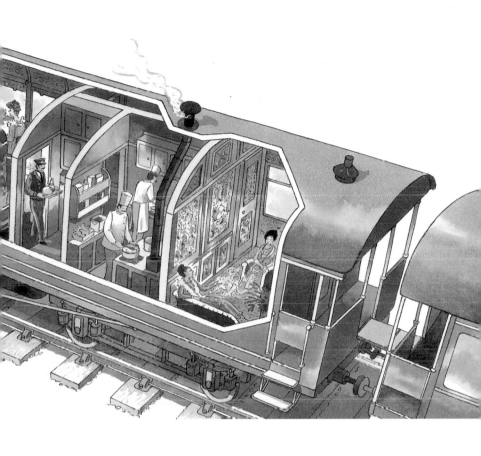

The *Orient Express* had splendid
compartments and even a library.
At night, servants made the seats
into beds with silk sheets. It was so
luxurious that passengers paid a
fortune for tickets.

Other companies joined in, offering every kind of carriage. People sat in comfortable compartments...

...or relaxed in saloon cars.

Some families booked a whole car just for themselves.

Best of all, people could buy food and drink. On the earliest trains, hungry passengers had to eat a quick meal at a station while the train waited for them.

Now trains had dining cars, things were much better – except when the train went over a bumpy track and food spilled everywhere.

If you couldn't afford an expensive ride, you could go on excursion trains. These took people on cheap trips from towns to the country or the seaside for a day.

Chapter 5

Faster and faster

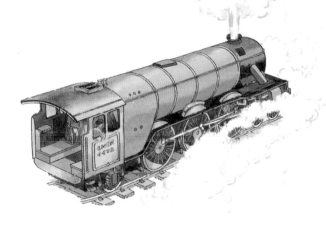

As train journeys became more popular, inventors began to try out different engines. This made the steam engineers panic and try to build even faster steam engines.

In the 1930s, an engineer named Gresley built *The Mallard*, the fastest steam engine ever. The front was smooth so the wind would rush over it. But steam engines already had a rival.

In 1892, Dr. Rudolf Diesel of Germany, had invented an engine that burned oil. Not only was it cheap and easy to run, it was also very fast.

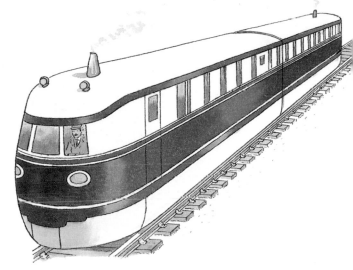

In 1939, a diesel train called the
Flying Hamburger set a new world
record for speed. Gradually, diesel
trains replaced steam engines. By
1965, most trains in America and
Europe were diesels.

The fastest trains in the world aren't diesels though. They are electric. The very first electric engine was built by Werner von Siemens in 1879.

He proudly showed it off at an exhibition in Berlin, Germany. Even though his engine was small, it easily carried over twenty people.

After the Second World War, when lots of tracks had been destroyed, new ones were built especially for electric trains.

They went so fast that people used them to go to and from work every day, even if they lived far away from their jobs.

Today, three kinds of train can travel at over 300km (200 miles) an hour. The first, in Japan, is shaped like a bullet and carries 115 million people across the country each year.

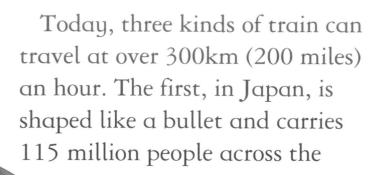

I haven't finished chapter one and we're nearly in Tokyo!

In Germany or China, you can take a *Maglev* train that floats above the rails.

Maglev trains are pulled along by magnets, with no noise or smoke at all.

And in France, you can ride on the *TGV*, the fastest passenger train in the world – so far...

Chapter 6

On the job

Trains are used all over the world, for all kinds of jobs. Many countries use vast freight trains to carry goods. One freight train in South Africa was over 600 wagons long.

Freight trains often take their loads all the way to the docks, where the crates are lifted straight onto ships.

Sometimes, the backs of whole trucks are loaded onto a freight train. The train gives the trucks a "piggy-back ride" to a station, where they are fixed to a truck engine and driven the rest of the way.

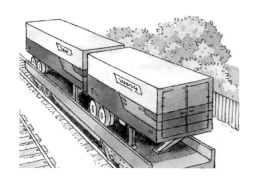

In hilly countries, trains have been designed to carry people up slopes. In 1870, a Swiss engineer built a railway up a mountain.

He put a third rail down the middle of the track and added a third wheel under the train. This gave the train an extra-strong grip as it went up and down.

Funiculars can crawl up even steeper slopes. Two carriages are fixed to a loop of metal cable, worked by steam or electricity. The weight of the carriage going down the slope helps to pull the other carriage up.

There are even trains designed to help other trains, by keeping rail tracks clean and safe.

Ballast cleaners clean the stones under the track...

...rail cranes pick
up obstacles...

...and snow
blowers clear
snow off
the line.

But most trains today carry
people – and, just like two
hundred years ago, people want
faster travel.

This is
like a roller
coaster!

So, trains have been invented
that tilt as they go around corners.
Other trains have to slow down
as they come to a bend or curve.
Tilting trains barely pause.

There are even some passenger trains that are run by computers. They don't have a driver at all.

Who's in charge?

Trains have come a long way since Richard Trevithick's engine, which he named *Catch-Me-Who-Can*, took people around and around in a circle.

Series editor: Lesley Sims

Designed by
Katarina Dragoslović

Based on original material by Caroline Young.
Original consultants: Mark Hambly & colleagues
(Llangollen Railway Society)
With thanks to D. Mosley (National Railway Museum, York)

This edition first published in 2007 by Usborne Publishing Ltd.,
Usborne House, 83-85 Saffron Hill, London EC1N 8RT, England.
www.usborne.com
Copyright © 2007, 2004, 1991 Usborne Publishing Ltd.